GLASGOW
OLD AND NEW

JACK HOUSE

Published by EP Publishing Limited 1974

Introduction

There can be hardly any city in the United Kingdom which is changing so completely and so rapidly as Glasgow. Exiled Glaswegians returning to the town on holiday are completely bewildered. Even people who knew Glasgow three or four years ago cannot recognise today the scenes which were so familiar to them then.

In its heyday Glasgow was the Second City of the Empire and one of the biggest in the world. Now it is the third biggest city in Britain, having had to give way to Birmingham as the second city of this country. According to Sir John Betjeman, Glasgow has the finest Victorian architecture to be found anywhere in the world. British architects, when they held a conference in Glasgow, confirmed this opinion.

But Glasgow Town Council decided to turn the place into the City of the Seventies. They had to start from scratch, because Glasgow, unlike other big centres in Britain, suffered very little from bombing during World War 2. They were obsessed—and now I give my own opinion—with the idea that the place should be made safe for the motor car, and this accounts for some of the surprising changes in the city.

In working out this book with my photographer, James Millar, we have been impressed by several factors. First of all, Glasgow, which remained more or less the same for many years, is now a place where things are either coming down or going up. Scaffolding is everywhere in the centre of the city.

Secondly, and this is perhaps more surprising, Glasgow is much greener than it used to be. There are various suggestions about the origin of the name Glasgow. I could provide you readily with a dozen, one from the Welsh and the rest from the Gaelic, the tongue spoken by Adam and Eve in the Garden of Eden, which was, as we all know, situated in the Western Isles of Scotland. At any rate, the favourite interpretation of Glasgow from the Town Council's point of view is "the dear green place".

The surprising thing, as I have indicated, is that this changing city becomes greener day by day. In the following pages you will see that certain scenes have been considerably changed by the growth of trees, plants and shrubs, and perhaps it's worth mentioning here that Glasgow, with 63 major parks and over 200 minor ones, has more parks per head of population than any city in Europe.

This picture book has been, to a large extent, dependent on the old prints and photographs which were available. We have collected them from a large number of sources—my own collection of Glasgow pictures, the Mitchell Library and other city libraries, the collection in the Art Department of "The Glasgow Herald" and the "Evening Times", and numerous other sources. I should mention especially that the scenes of Anderston Cross were from postcards in the possession of Charles Capaldi, loaned to the Shandon Buttery Restaurant at Anderston.

One of the biggest difficulties in the making of this book has been to try to take the modern photographs from as nearly as possible the same angle as the original photograph or print. I must record that James Millar has performed amazing feats of derring-do in order to achieve this. In some cases it has been impossible because the physical scenery has changed so much.

I hope you will agree that this picture book is evocative of Glasgow Old and New. Ever since Will Fyffe first sang "I belong to Glasgow, dear old Glasgow town"—a song which has gone right round the world and has even been translated into Russian—people have been interested in this remarkable city, and not only Glaswegians but visitors who were astonished by what they found in the place.

So this book is a record of a changing city and, as far as I know, it is the only one which shows both the old and the new. I hope it will appeal to Glaswegians not only in Glasgow but all over the world.

Jack House
Glasgow, August, 1974

Note on the Author
JACK HOUSE

Jack House is literary editor of the Glasgow Evening Times and author of some 30 books on Glasgow and the Clyde. He works also for the Scottish Lecture Agency and has given lectures all over Britain. The author is a well-known figure in Glasgow and for the past 22 years has been a member of the Scottish team in BBC Radio's "Round Britain Quiz". Jack House has a great love for the city of Glasgow and is the ideal man to compile such a book.

Contents

George Square - 1870

The original centre of the city was Glasgow Cross, but George Square gradually took over. The square was built over a little loch and laid out with gardens, surrounded by hotels, dwelling houses and offices. The statue of Sir Walter Scott is the centre piece and a few other statues can be seen, including (left of centre) Queen Victoria, on horseback.

1

George Square - 1974

Some of the statues are still there, but the scene has changed. In the background are the ornate Italian style City Chambers and the top of the Cenotaph can be seen above the trees. James Watt is still in the foreground, but Queen Victoria is now on the other side of the Information Bureau on the left. The equestrian statue portrays Prince Albert. In the background are the new buildings of the University of Strathclyde.

George Square - 1901
The City Chambers is the biggest brick building in Glasgow, although most people don't realise that. The facings are of stone but the erection behind is of brick. Note the hansom and other cabs and, on the left, the cabmen's shelter, which lasted until 1920.

3

George Square - 1974
The trees have grown in 70 years. The Square is more open. Buses and cars have replaced the horse-drawn cabs.
And the old gas lamps (now much sought after by house-owners) are replaced by tall electric standards.

George Square from the South East - early 1800's
This print shows the Square in the 1820s when only one statue (Sir John Moore, seen in the background, left) had been erected. There are 12 of them now! Most of the buildings were hotels or dwelling places owned by people well enough off to have their own coaches.

George Square from the South East - 1974
The Bank of Scotland and the Merchants' House, with its dome, dominate the view today. Sir Walter Scott has arrived in the centre. To the right is the partly new North British Hotel. And the shop on the extreme right has been replaced by the City Chambers. On the extreme left, the General Post Office.

Queen Street - early 19th century
On the left is the headquarters of the Royal Bank of Scotland. The house formerly belonged to one of the Glasgow Tobacco Lords, William Cunninghame of Lainshaw. On the right the pillared building is the Theatre Royal, the first theatre in Britain to be illuminated by gas!

Queen Street - 1974

William Cunninghame's house still stands on the left, but Corinthian pillars have been built at the front when it became the Royal Exchange. The continuation of the building behind the mansion was the hall of the Exchange. The whole is now Stirling's Library. On the right, behind the scaffolding, there are still the pillars of the Theatre Royal.

Buchanan Street from St. Enoch Square - 1906
Horse-drawn traffic ruled the roost at the beginning of this century. Only two motor vehicles can be readily observed in this scene – the private car in the foreground and the Fry's Chocolate van left of centre in the background.

Buchanan Street from St. Enoch Square - 1974
Pedestrian precincts have taken over, both in St. Enoch Square (immediate foreground) and Buchanan Street.
Observe that Samuel the jewellers are still at the same corner of Buchanan Street and Argyle Street. The only
horses seen in Buchanan Street today are those of the mounted police.

Buchanan Street, looking north - 1911
Though tram-cars seemed to be everywhere in Glasgow at the start of the century, they were not allowed in Buchanan Street, which was the city's most distinguished shopping centre. Note the boy admiring the up-to-date horseless carriage.

Buchanan Street, looking north - 1974
The buildings have hardly changed at all in the last 60 odd years, although away in the background you can see the Chevalier Casino in place of the low tenements. Some of the buildings are being considerably altered, notably the Fraser warehouse on the left, behind the barricades. This street becomes a pedestrian precinct from 11 a.m. and the presence of the car in the foreground shows that the photograph was taken earlier.

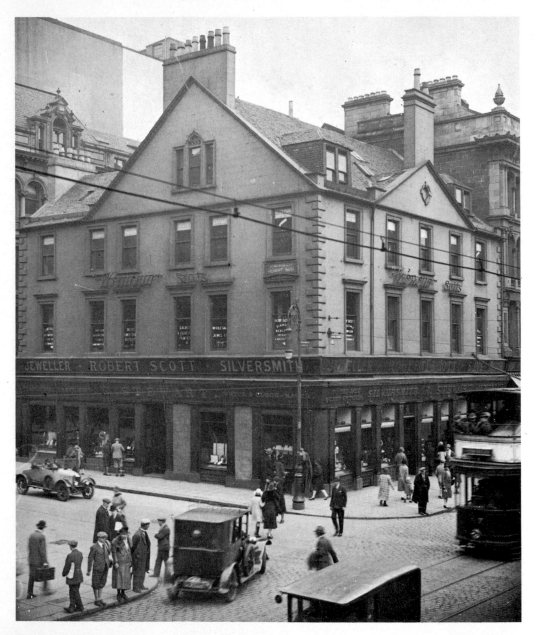

Corner of Buchanan Street and Argyle Street - 1923
A taxi turns into Buchanan Street just behind a tram-car which was open back and front on the upper deck. Note the gentlemen wearing plus fours, de rigeur for casual wear in the Twenties.

Corner of Buchanan Street and Argyle Street - 1974
Taxis can't turn into Buchanan Street today because it is a pedestrian precinct. Burton's building has replaced the old shops. There are no tram-lines, but motor vehicles are not allowed to stop in the tartan patterned place in the foreground. Plus fours seem to have disappeared for ever.

Buchanan Street, looking south - 1871

This was the less fashionable end of Buchanan Street, which only got really posh after St. George's-in-the-Fields Church, centre background. From there down to St. Enoch's Church, far background, were clubs, expensive shops and Italian warehousemen.

15

Buchanan Street, looking south - 1974
After more than 100 years there have been few changes in the buildings on the right hand side. The Waverley Temperance Hotel is now the Ivanhoe (licensed) Hotel. The Royal Scottish Academy of Music has replaced the tenements between the hotel and the kirk, and the Stock Exchange has been built on the other side. St. Enoch's Church has disappeared.

St. Vincent Place - 1912
St. Vincent Place saw plenty of tram-cars (better known as ''the caurs'') for it was a switching area as well as having through lines. The buildings on the left are the Clydesdale Bank, the ''Citizen'' office, the Anchor Line office and the Bank of Scotland. The City Chambers are in the background.

St. Vincent Place - 1974
St. Vincent Place looks much the same as it did in 1912, even to the gentlemen's lavatory, though the ornate lamp standard in front of it has been replaced by a soulless electrical post. The Clydesdale Bank is still on the left, but the other offices are in different hands.

George Street - 1922

George Street was a respectable residential area but by the time this picture was taken it was going down in the world. The tall building on the right was owned by a cigarette-making firm. Behind the church spire can be seen one of the domes of the City Chambers.

George Street - 1974
Urban renewal has caused most of the old tenements to disappear. Behind the remains on the left is part of the block formerly owned by the "Scottish Daily Express". The trees now visible are in the Ramshorn kirkyard. The church has disappeared, and the modern building on the right is part of Strathclyde University.

Gordon Street - 1911
Gordon Street was the first sight of Glasgow for many a visitor who arrived at the Central Station on the right. In the good old summer-time men wore straw hats, as you can see, and awnings protected shop windows from the glare. The Greek Thomson building on the left was the famous Grosvenor Restaurant.

Gordon Street - 1974

Architecturally, Gordon Street has not changed one whit in 60 years, though the scaffolding on the left suggests that changes may be coming. A traffic policeman is now unnecessary and men-about-town prefer bare heads to straw bashers. And the famous Grosvenor, affected by fire, has been standing empty for years.

Union Street, looking north - 1914
Rush-hour in Glasgow. As you can see by the clock it's 5 p.m., and the workers of the world, plus shopping housewives, are making for trams to take them home to the Glasgow suburbs. The man standing in the way of the Springburn tram (foreground) is not courting death. He is a tramway employee who keeps tram crossings free of grit.

Union Street, looking north - 1974
Boots' new store now dominates the scene. Their clock shows 10.30 a.m. and there's no rush. The tramlines have gone. Many of the buildings, notably those on extreme right and left, are new. The sheds in Union Street mark the workings where a new sewer is being laid and this partly accounts for the lack of traffic.

West Nile Street - 1930
A familiar sight in West Nile Street until the Second World War was the line of trace-horses waiting to assist horse-drawn lorries up the steep incline to the north. The figures in the doorway on the right are trace-boys awaiting a job. The Clydesdales were owned by Glasgow Corporation and won many prizes at horse shows.

West Nile Street - 1974

You'll hardly see a horse in the centre of Glasgow nowadays, though there are still plenty on the perimeter.
The motor has taken over completely in this view. There are new buildings on the left. But farther down the scene
remains unchanged, with the Charles Rennie Mackintosh tower of the "Glasgow Herald and Evening Times"
building in the background to the right.

Morrison's Court, Argyle Street - 1931
Morrison's Court is one of the oldest parts of Argyle Street and it was here that John Morrison built his eating house. "Arcade Cafe" signifies the old entrance, changed to the back door when the new entrance was made in the Argyll Arcade, opened in 1828.

27

Morrison's Court, Argyle Street - 1974
The scene has hardly changed in over 40 years, except that there's no horse in the background and the cars are different. The cobbles look unchanged, but the new owners of the restaurant have brightened up the frontage considerably. It is the oldest restaurant existing in Glasgow.

St. Enoch Square - 1929
Ironically, this picture was taken to show the St. Enoch Subway Station, proposed for demolition to widen the bottleneck into Argyle Street and Buchanan Street. The station is now regarded as a piece of Late Victorian architecture worth preserving, and the Subway is to be extended. Also ironically, this picture is taken from St. Enoch Station, which is to be demolished.

St. Enoch Square - 1974

So far from opening the bottle-neck, the authorities have now completely closed it to through traffic. Trees and shrubs have been planted. The line of taxis reminds us that this Square was famous in the 18th century for its line of sedan chairs carried by stalwart Highlanders. There are new buildings to right and left of the bottle-neck, and behind the dome one of the cranes, now ubiquitous in Glasgow, can be seen.

Trongate - 1914
One of the eight streets of Glasgow which Daniel Defoe saw in the 18th century, the Trongate has two venerable buildings—on the right the steeple of Tron-St. Mary's Church and in the distance, left of centre, the Tolbooth Steeple, built in 1626. Note the open-upper-deck tramcar and the line of billboard men on the right.

Trongate - 1974

Architecturally, the scene has not changed much in 60 years. The Glasgow Cross railway station is no longer in use and its dome has gone. So has the statue of William of Orange (better known in Glasgow as "King Billy"), now to be seen in Cathedral Square. Buildings beyond the Cross have been demolished, and the tram-lines were lifted 12 years ago.

Trongate, looking west - 1901
This view of the Trongate is interesting from the sartorial point of view. A typical Glasgow "shawlie" is seen in the right foreground. On the left is the Glasgow Cross railway station, and just above the heads of the passengers on the Ibrox tram you can see King Billy on his horse. He was portrayed as a Roman emperor.

Trongate, looking west - 1974
The Glasgow Cross railway station has long since closed. Buses run along a one-way street where trams once glided both ways. King Billy has gone to Cathedral Square. But the buildings, including the steeple of Tron-St. Mary's kirk, are substantially unaltered.

The Bridgegate, looking towards Saltmarket - circa. 1870
The Bridgegate was a once fashionable street which went down in the world. Obviously the inhabitants did not take kindly to photographers. This is where many of the Irish immigrants settled when they had left their native isle during the "Hungry Forties".

The Bridgegate, looking towards Saltmarket - 1974
A railway bridge has been built over the Bridgegate and some of the old tenements on the left are coming down, an indication of extensive demolition. On the right is Shipbank Lane and the people entering it are going to shop in "Paddy's Market", which has a direct relationship with the poor Irish who made the Briggait their centre.

Richmond Street - 1930

When well-to-do Glaswegians left the Glasgow Cross area for better housing, many of them settled in Richmond Street and in adjacent thoroughfares. Note the pillared entrance to the house on the right. Cobbled streets existed in Glasgow until a few years ago, and occasionally a bit of one may still be seen.

37

Richmond Street - 1974
The modern buildings of the University of Strathclyde have replaced the modest terrace, and students stroll where city merchants and shopkeepers once walked. By the time the University plans are completed, this whole area will have been changed completely.

East Clyde Street, looking west - 1914
A morning scene outside the Glasgow Fish Market, on the right. The picture was taken from under the Glasgow and South Western Railway bridge across the Clyde, leading into St. Enoch Station. Tram-cars are crossing Victoria Bridge. Apart from them, the traffic is almost entirely horse-drawn.

Clyde Street, looking west - 1974
The "East" has long been dropped from the name of the street. The Fish Market still operates, but not on the scale that it did once. Trees almost hide the Victoria Bridge. And the railway bridge no longer carries trains into St. Enoch Station, which is now a car park.

Clyde Street - about 1820

Joseph Swan, who made this engraving, cheated a bit in this view of the north bank of the River Clyde. It shows on the right the Town's Hospital and Poorhouse, built in 1733. In the centre stands the new Catholic Chapel, completed in 1817. The horses and carts in the foreground - or forewater! - show how shallow the river could be at this point.

Clyde Street - 1974

The camera shows a more realistic view across the Clyde. The only old building which remains is the Catholic Chapel, now St. Andrew's Cathedral. Warehouses stand on either side and in front is the new river walkway. On the right is the sailing ship "Carrick", now the R.N.V.R. Club. The river is deeper and is occasionally dredged.

Bridge Street Railway Station - 1939
This was the original main railway station in Glasgow and stood on the south side of the River Clyde not far from Jamaica Street Bridge. It was superseded when the Central Station was built on the north side of the river. When this picture was taken, the pillared entrance and adjoining buildings were all that was left of the station.

Site of Bridge Street Station - 1974
The station entrance has been demolished (despite pleas from railway enthusiasts) and the site is used as a car park until a new building is erected. In the background is the bridge which carries the railway over the Clyde to Central Station with the electric rail equipment showing above the parapet.

Corner of Broomielaw and Jamaica Street - 1914

Paisley's Corner has been famous in Glasgow for well over 100 years. A single motor car moves grimly through the horse traffic and a tram-car in Jamaica Street waits for a chance to cross. On the left is the railway into Central Station and the hoardings show that holidays in Nice and Monte Carlo were being offered to Glaswegians in 1914.

45

Corner of Broomielaw and Jamaica Street - 1974
Although it looks considerably brighter, Paisley's Corner has changed very little in 60 years. The shop windows and fascia have been modernised, but architecturally it remains the same group of buildings. There are more differences in the railway into Central Station, where signs of electrification can be seen.

The Broomielaw, looking west - 1920

When this picture was taken the Broomielaw was the place from which the Firth of Clyde sailings took place. On the left can be seen the signs showing destinations (Rothesay and Benmore) and steamer names (''Lord of the Isles''). Ships from England, Ireland and farther afield discharged goods here, as can be seen by the variety of lorries. The River Clyde is behind the buildings on the left.

The Broomielaw, looking west - 1974

Ships and steamers no longer come as far up the Clyde as the Broomielaw. The steamer sheds have been replaced by a Traffic Control Computer Centre for the Glasgow streets. Many buildings on the right hand side have been demolished and replaced. The only nautical touch left is the frontage of the restaurant below the whisky sign on the right.

Glasgow Harbour - 1895
Ships of all kinds thronged into the River Clyde at Glasgow in Victorian days. As much traffic and goods came in by river as came in by rail. Farther down river were the famous Clyde shipyards, where the shipbuilders claimed to turn out the biggest and best ships in the world.

Glasgow Harbour - 1974
The only shipping seen in the upper reaches of Glasgow Harbour now are dredgers and police launches. In the background you see the new Kingston Bridge which has considerably altered cross-river traffic. Behind the bridge if the Iron Ore Terminal, where big ships still come in to deposit iron ore.

THE CLYDE, GLASGOW, FROM SAILORS HOME.

The Clyde from Sailors' Home, Broomielaw - 1900
Passenger steamers comprise most of the shipping seen at the Broomielaw side and at the Bridge Wharf on the other side. They took a multitude of people "doon the watter" every summer. The nearest railway bridges take trains into the Central Station on the left. Other Clyde bridges can be seen in the background.

The Clyde from Sailors' Home - 1974
It was not possible to take this picture from the same angle as the one on the opposite page, but it can be seen that the river is empty. In front of the Central Station railway bridge is the George V Bridge for motor and pedestrian traffic. A river walkway is planned to take the place of the old sheds.

Glassford Street - 1828

Joseph Swan did this engraving especially to show the Trades House of Glasgow, the building on the right with dome. It is an Adam building and the only one in Glasgow still used for its original purpose, the meeting of the Incorporations of the Trades of the city. As you can see, they were digging up streets even then!

Glassford Street - 1974
Nearly 150 years later the Trades House is the only 1828 building still in existence in Glassford Street. On the extreme right, undergoing a face lift, are the headquarters of the Savings Bank of Glasgow. New warehouses run down both sides of Glassford Street, but here and there some century old buildings are still in use.

Ingram Street, looking west - 1828
John Knox a distinguished Glasgow artist, made this drawing of Ingram Street soon after the rebuilding of the Ramshorn Kirk on the right. The street had been widened, as can be seen by the demolition of a protruding house, extreme right. The tower of Hutcheson's Hospital is in the centre and at the end of the street is the Tobacco Lord's mansion which is now part of Stirling's Library.

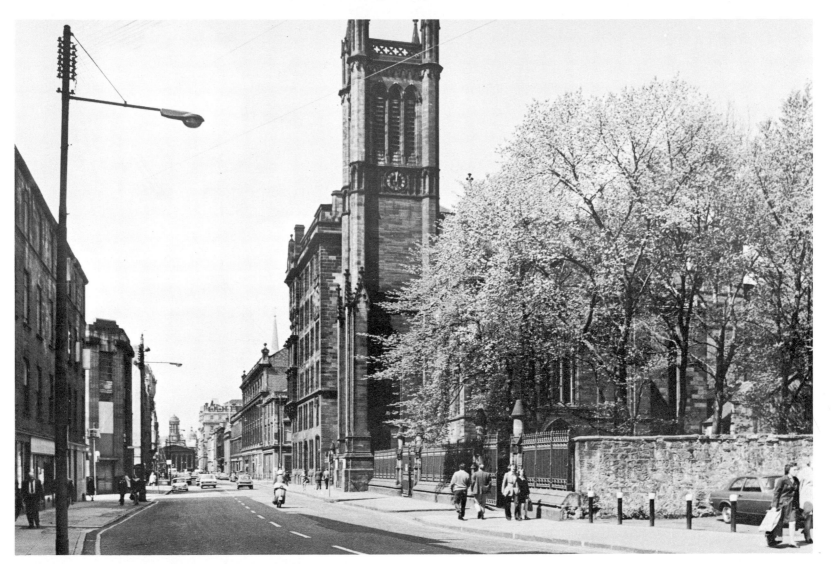

Ingram Street, looking west - 1974
Glasgow is known as "the dear green place" and you can see why when you look at the growth of the trees round the Ramshorn Kirk. New warehouses have got into the way of the view of the Hutchesons' Hospital tower. And the Corinthian pillars and clock tower of Stirling's Library replaces the view of the Tobacco Lord's house.

Glasgow from the Fir Park - 1828
The Fir Park became the Necropolis in 1832, but it was a pleasant place of resort in 1828. On the right is the Cathedral and a funeral is taking place in the kirkyard. This engraving shows the western clock tower and consistory house, both of which were later removed.

Glasgow from the Necropolis - 1974
As nearly as possible this photograph shows the scene from the same point as the artist's. But he used artistic licence and went much farther than the camera could. The oldest house in Glasgow (Provand's Lordship, 15th century) can be seen peeping round a tree left of the chimney stalk.

39784. Glasgow Necropolis. F.F.& Co.

The Necropolis - 1901

The Necropolis, standing beside Glasgow Cathedral, is the burying ground of the Merchants' House of Glasgow and was opened in 1832. The vaults in the foreground are actually within the Cathedral confines. The statue on the hill is that of John Knox, the Reformer. His expression as he looks over the city is a severe one.

The Necropolis - 1974
Once again here is evidence that Glasgow is "the dear green place". Foliage almost obliterates the view of the Necropolis, though John Knox looks grimmer than ever. The object in the left foreground is a mort-safe, used to prevent the body-snatchers from stealing coffins and corpses.

Sauchiehall Street - 1954
Taken from the roof of La Scala Cinema, this picture shows Sauchiehall Street when tram-cars were beginning to lose their ascendancy – though not in this street, apparently. The building in the right background was the new N.A.A.F.I. The one on the left was Green's Playhouse, once the biggest cinema in Europe.

Sauchiehall Street - 1974

Twenty years later and Sauchiehall Street is dwarfed by a new high-rise office block where the Y.M.C.A. used to be. The N.A.A.F.I. is now the Chevalier Casino, Green's Playhouse is the Apollo Centre, with high-rise flats on the skyline, and where the tram-cars ran is now a pedestrian precinct.

39763. Glasgow. Sauchiehall Street F.F&Cº

Sauchiehall Street - 1900

Though it achieved world-wide fame as a shopping centre and fashionable thoroughfare, Sauchiehall Street was a late starter and, although this picture shows some imposing warehouses and other buildings, there were still mansion houses with gardens just over the hill. It was the way to the West End and so became an exclusive street until Buchanan Street bested it.

Sauchiehall Street - 1974

This part of Sauchiehall Street is now a pedestrian precinct, though it suffers somewhat from the fact that two of Glasgow's best stores, Copland and Lye's and Pettigrew and Stephen's have been demolished and are not yet replaced. Quite a number of the buildings are the same as 74 years ago—the one on the right corner, the former Gaumont Cinema covered in scaffolding, and one or two others farther up the street.

Sauchiehall Street, west end - 1900

At the west end of Sauchiehall Street there were still private houses in their own gardens in 1900. From them there were views right to Kelvingrove Park in the west. The tower of the Theological College can be seen in the right background. Sauchiehall Street at this end was mainly residential.

Sauchiehall Street, west end - 1974
The place has changed so much that it's difficult to orientate oneself. But there are clues in the tenements bottom left, and in the church spire. Everywhere new buildings have gone up and, you can see from the cranes, are still ascending.

Charing Cross - 1888

In 1888 Glasgow's first great Exhibition was held in Kelvingrove Park. We see the head of the Royal procession marching to the opening ceremony. In the background is Albany Place, a row of terrace houses later to be hidden by new warehouses and flats. The Grand Hotel, suitably decorated, is on the left.

Charing Cross - 1974

You may find difficulty in relating this picture to the one on the opposite page but it is the same scene taken from the same angle. The flower plots mark the place where the Grand Hotel once stood. Behind are Charing Cross Mansions, where Albany Place used to be. A motorway runs under Charing Cross now.

Charing Cross - 1901
Charing Cross Mansions have now obliterated Albany Place, but are still dominated by the Grand Hotel, which was regarded as the most fashionable hotel in Glasgow at that time. The Charing Cross Fountain actually worked in those days!

Charing Cross - 1974

The changes at Charing Cross are more readily identifiable from this picture because the Fountain on the left and Charing Cross Mansions centre right are obvious pinpoints. The new looking building on the right is the Baird Hall of Residence of Strathclyde University. It was built as a hotel in 1938.

39757 Glasgow.Kelvingrove Park. F.F.&Co.

Kelvingrove Park - 1870

Kelvingrove Park was the scene of the great Glasgow Exhibitions of 1888, 1901 and 1911. Behind Kelvingrove House, to the right of the Stewart Fountain, lies the western end of Sauchiehall Street.

Kelvingrove Park - 1974
Here's yet another case of "the dear green place" affecting a view. The statue of the tigress in the foreground and the fountain, and the distant view of Sauchiehall Street, are all that we can see in the summer. The tigress, by the way, was given to Glasgow by an American Glaswegian and a replica stands in Central Park, New York.

Kelvingrove House - before 1900
Kelvingrove House stood by the River Kelvin in the midst of an estate which was bought by Glasgow Corporation and turned into Kelvingrove Park. This picture was taken when it was still privately owned. The house was demolished in 1900.

Site of Kelvingrove House - 1974
This is the nearest approximation we could make to the site of Kelvingrove House. The River Kelvin can be seen behind the trees on the right. Across the roller skating rink are the grounds of Glasgow University, and its tower rises on the skyline.

Old Kelvin Bridge - before 1900
This picture was taken to show the River Kelvin in spate, but it also shows the original Kelvin Bridge which joined Glasgow to the Burgh of Hillhead. The new bridge was built above the old one, which was still in use. In this picture Glasgow is on the left and Hillhead on the right. The tower of Glasgow University can be seen dimly on the left.

Kelvinbridge - 1974

It was impossible to photograph the site of the Old Kelvin Bridge from the angle the original photographer used, so this picture shows the new Kelvinbridge from the opposite side. The old bridge crossed diagonally under the new one. The spire of Lansdowne Church, on the right, is said to be the second slimmest in Europe.

Woodside Place - 1901
Coming up from Sauchiehall Street in the old days you saw the tall tower of the Theological College, with its two attendant towers to the east, and the opposing tower of Park Church on the left. The story goes that one religious body tried to outdo the other. Everything is very trim and quiet at this time.

Woodside Place - 1974

The trees have taken over yet again. So have the motor cars. The dear quiet place has become a dear busy place with cars parked as far as the eye can reach. The Park Church tower is embowered in foliage, which is maybe just as well because the tower is all that remains of the church.

Hyndland - the turn of the century
Suburbia, not even quite close suburbia, is seldom commemorated. Here is a view, taken at the turn of the century, of the area which is now Hyndland. On the high ground to the left is Gartnavel Mental Hospital, a bright and shining new building then. On the right is Hyndland Church, with Hyndland railway station near by.

Hyndland - 1974
This scene has been photographed from approximately the same position as the old one. The new terraces have blotted out the pastoral aspect and even the former landmarks. The only point of contact is the roof of Hyndland Church, which can be seen peeping over the rooftops to the left of the other church tower. It's a moot point whether the view is better or not.

Great Western Road, Anniesland - c.1945
Reasons for pictures are often as interesting as the pictures themselves. This was taken to show the "bottle-neck" at Anniesland on the Great Western Road. It was proposed to eliminate it at a cost of £37,000. The bridge leads to a railway station on the right.

Great Western Road, Anniesland - 1974
Here we see the effect on the "bottle-neck" of the widening of the road. Something has been trimmed off the right side of the bridge but otherwise it looks much the same. A cinema has been built where there was only waste ground on the right. The railway bridge is better. And there are more trees.

Castlebank Street, Partick - 1890

Partick was an old village when Glasgow was still growing up. These thatched buildings, one of them crowstepped, belong to old Partick. "New" tenements have been built uncomfortably alongside them. Castlebank Street takes its name after the Bishop's Castle on the banks of the River Kelvin, to which he repaired on holiday.

Castlebank Street, Partick - 1974
Only one of the tenements remains of the old Castlebank Street. Buildings have been swept away to give access to the new Expressway which runs along the side of the river Clyde to the left. The cranes of shipbuilding yards can be seen in the background, but whether or not they are being used is another matter.

Anderston Cross, looking east - 1920
The village of Anderston was once a weaving place outside Glasgow. There was, until recent years, a boundary
stone on the right hand side of Argyle Street (seen here) which marked your entry into Anderston from Glasgow.
The area, looking reasonably prosperous here, went down as the years went by.

Anderston Cross, looking east - 1974
This, believe it or not, is the same scene from the same angle as the picture opposite. There was, as you will see opposite, a railway station at Anderston Cross and in the foreground you can still see the platform in a tunnel. This is now one of Glasgow's ''spaghetti junctions''. In the new buildings in the background is housed Radio Clyde.

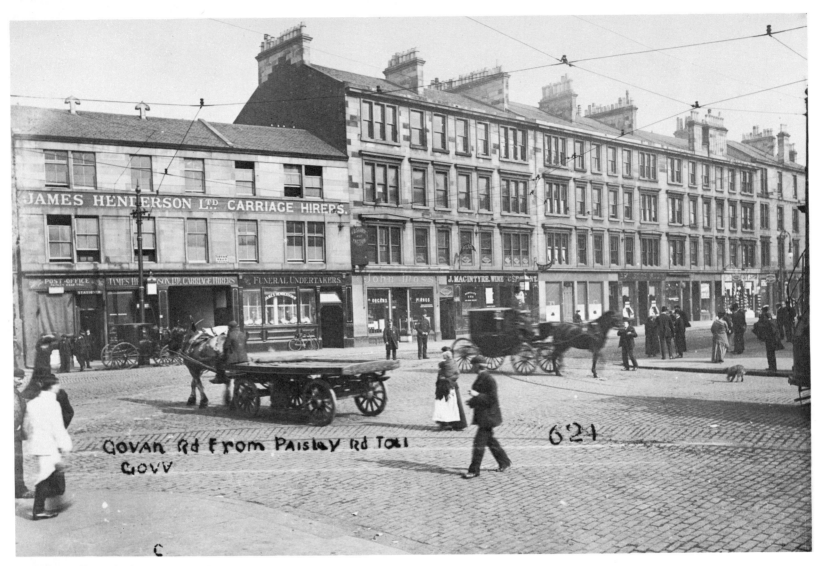

Paisley Road Toll - 1890

The ubiquitous horse of Victorian days is again in evidence. Even the end of the tram-car, seen on the extreme right, shows it's a horse-drawn one. The equipage to the right of centre belongs to a well-known doctor in the district.

Paisley Road Toll - 1974
There have been few architectural changes in this street scene. The tenements in the background remain the same, though the shops have been brightened up. The carriage hirer's building is essentially the same, but has been tarted up to be a cinema, a bingo hall, and a club. The lack of traffic is accounted for by the road work going on.

EAST SIDE OF WATER ROW, GOVAN. 24TH MAY 1861.

Water Row, Govan - 1861

Water Row led from Govan Cross down to the River Clyde, and it must be remembered that Govan kept itself clear from Glasgow for many years. Even today Govanites regard themselves as quite different from Glaswegians. The tavern shown here was a regular port of call for travellers who were going to board the steamers at Govan Pier.

Water Row, Govan - 1974
From the ornamental fountain at Govan Cross we look at what remains of the modern Water Row. There are no old houses left and on the right demolition is being carried out on buildings leading to the Clyde. Even the famous Govan Ferry, which carried people and vehicles across the river, has gone.

Govan Parish Church Kirkyard - 1920

Govan Parish Church is on the site of a Druids' temple, and in the grounds and the church are some of the finest examples of burial memorials to be found in Britain. In some cases there are stones with heathen inscriptions on one side and Christian inscriptions on the other. The tombstones in this picture are more modern. In the background is the Pearce Institute.

Govan Parish Church Kirkyard - 1974
Little seems to have changed in the last 50 or so years in Govan Parish Church Kirkyard. But, if you look carefully, you can see what the weather and vandals can accomplish in the way of destruction. Of the tallest memorial only the plinth and some scattered stones are left, and all that remains of the strong railings in the central tomb are the posts.

Battle of Langside Memorial - 1888
Mary Queen of Scots was defeated by the Regent Moray at the Battle of Langside in the 16th century. This monument was erected at the top of the hill where her generals finally gave in. In the nearby Langside Public Library you can learn all about the Battle.

Battle of Langside Memorial - 1974
Langside has grown from a village into an important Glasgow suburb since the Battle Memorial was erected. The crossing is now an important road junction. There is a fine church opposite the Memorial, and in the background can be seen buildings, stretching from left to right, of the renowned Victoria Infirmary,

Old Cathcart - 1870
Cathcart was an old village outside Glasgow, but it is now within the city boundaries. Up the road in this picture is the Court Knowe, across from Cathcart Castle, and it was here that Mary Queen of Scots sat and watched her army being defeated at the Battle of Langside. The road to the right takes you to an ancient bridge and the old Cathcart Snuff Mill.

Old Cathcart - 1974
Cathcart is one of the pleasantest of Glasgow suburbs (although true Cathcart supporters still think of it as a place apart) and has a fine park attached to it. Here and there efforts have been made to preserve the old buildings. Careful examination will show that the buildings on the left are part of the old cottages in the facing picture. They are being turned into modern residences behind the ancient frontage.

Crossmyloof Row, Strathbungo - Late Victorian

Strathbungo (over whose name arguments still blaze) was a village on its own but, like so many others, it was taken over by Glasgow. This row of old cottages stood just opposite Crossmyloof railway station. You can see the board advertising the station on the right.

Moray Place, Strathbungo - 1974
The famous Glasgow architect known as "Greek" Thomson came to Strathbungo and transformed Crossmyloof Row into elegant terraces. This shows the start of a fine series of houses. The remains of Crossmyloof railway station are still on the right, but the station ceased to operate many years ago. Strathbungo is now regarded as a "preservation" area.

This edition first published 1974
by EP Publishing Limited
East Ardsley, Wakefield, Yorkshire
England

ISBN: 0 7158 1078 2

ep

Please address all enquiries to EP Publishing Limited
(address as above)

Printed in Great Britain by Fretwell & Brian Limited
Silsden, Keighley, Yorkshire.